The Brazilian Exodus

The Brazilian Exodus

By

Robert L. Morgan

Dedication:

This Story is dedicated to my son Caleb, for he was the inspiration for the exodus, we joked around while playing one-on-one basketball. While in the Persian Gulf during the second Gulf War, I wrote the majority of this story and added to it over time as inspiration hit me.

In the 21 century, science will embrace environmentalism and be the catalyst to solving and eliminating pollution. The world will finally have clean air, clean water and wild life will be preserved.

"people of earth have united, Clean Air and Water, the protection of endangered species and of the rain forest"
"Mother Earth saved and oxygen for all"!

'For Mother Earth is Queen and she has mandated that we preserve her at all cost: Clean Air/Water and the preservation of the species-plants and animals. To sacrifice humanity to protect her wild life is accepted and even demanded, it is our service to her, in return for the natural resources we use to build our cities'.

In 2043:

"Colonial, positive ID of humanoids in sector 37".

"On Display! O.k. now relay the satellite data to airborne recon." Immediately an AR-45 was dispatched to sector 37 and then received precise GPS coordinates of the unauthorized (UA) inhabitants in South America. It was necessary to use an AR-45 instead of just blasting the UAs from space with a powerful laser, for it could be another wayward scientist or government official having a liaison in the unpopulated continent of South America.

"AR-45 to bio-enforcement center 29, positive ID of a group of 20 unauthorized"

"Very well AR-45, deploy your extraction team, and warm up your airborne laser for backup".

"AR-45 to center, request confirmation of the use of ABL into the Rain Forest"

"Confirmed, this is Colonial Blake, regional commander, you are authorized to use the ABL into the rain forest in support of the extraction team". "Gentlemen, lets wrap this up today, we have lost too many good men in this operation. As you all know this is our finest hour and mankind's noblest venture, the preservation of the Rain Forest and the protection of endangered species."

The extraction team rapidly departed the aircraft and gracefully glided to their target, utilizing GPS data that was linked to their helmet cams. This highly mobile and lethal team has the state of the art weaponry, each with a mobile computer that is linked to SATCOM data, and receives digital imagery from the AR-45, which is also linked to each member. Each member's M-22 assault rifle is linked to his computer and all data is displayed on their helmet visor. The team quickly found the group of UAs, another group of indigenous' who refused the world's mandate to evacuate South America. As the team approached the group of 20, they tried to escape, the first 15 were eliminated, and the remaining five or so put up some resistance. They holed up in a small rock out cropping and had a few crude rockets, once the first rocket was fired, the sensors on AR-45 picked it up, and its computer system automatically locked on and fired its ABL. Even though the aircraft was now a good 50 miles away this powerful laser decimated the remaining five holdouts.

Normally the A.B.L. system, which originally came into being in 2005, was used to shot down ballistic missiles, but now it use to assist in the Brazilian Exodus. The use of any airborne laser into the rain forest is restricted and must have proper authorization, for protecting mother earth is ever citizen's ultimate responsibility. These highly powerful and accurate lasers have a range of well over 200 miles, and are normally used to shot down poachers, and occasionally eco-

terrorist try to shoot a discarded ICMB (with no warhead) into South America to protest the removal of all indigenous people.

"AR-45 to bio-enforcement center 29, mission completed"

"BZ, team, I'll inform the UN that the Brazilian Exodus in now complete"

The last indigenous people of South America has left the continent and moved to newly erected towered cites. These towers are enormously large and extremely tall, like a needle piercing the heavens; sky scrappers have nothing on these buildings. Each building is a city in themselves, each with its own schools, hospitals, grocery stores, malls, gyms, libraries, movie theaters and chapels for various faiths, places of employment and of course housing for 50,000 to 100, 000 people.

These massive city towers are knows as millennium buildings, each with its own designation, currently M500 is being built in Toronto.

The concept for these 'M's' as they are commonly known as, was originally an engineer's/futurist's dream; the first one to be built was in 2020 in Tokyo, Japan. A marvel of modern engineering, this one building alone used the equivalent of Japan's annual supply of steel. In view of the fact that this building project was so successful, not only from the engineering standpoint, but from the habitability aspect—one building can now easily house 50, 000 people. Moreover, with large underground networks and adjacent buildings the capacity almost doubles.

Now that housing a great mass of people has been solved, and the political and environmental climate as it was, it was decided to finally solve the rain forest problem of South America. For the left wing, environmentalists now controlled all the governments around the world. Since the people of earth have united, at least on this one theme: Clean Air and Water, the protection of endangered species and of course the rain forest. For it was the common belief that if the rain forest 'is not protected and allowed to grow', the world would start running out of oxygen.

******

Cold Fusion

There was only one major obstacle left to solve, Energy. The concept of large Bio-zones of people all living in cities of the futures, in multiple M-type towers with energy efficient transportation systems linking them together, without abundant power would never work. For the second aspect of this plan was to eliminate the automobile and most combustion engines, which in turn would cut down on pollution and in time the world would have clean air.

On the morning of July 18, 2025, the world moved into a new era, for **Nuclear Fusion** *(Cold Fusion—the binding of two atoms to create or form a large atom, energy binding) finally became a reality, clean energy without nuclear waste. Since this was a joint international venture this new technology was not horded, all the major nations of the world started building them.*

In time, nuclear proliferation will be a thing of the past, for there was no more weapons grade plutonium or uranium. It did not happen over night, but since no nation would be depending on another for fossil fuels, OPEC had to get with the times or be left behind. For it seems that money and their lack of it out weighed their religious rhetoric.

In a few short years self-sufficient bio-zones were built, first in the major cities like, New York, Chicago, Detroit, LA, Paris and Moscow. Most large businesses recognize the warning sign and shifted from the automobile industry over to mass transportation or to the numerous internal equipment needed to make a tower city operate. For in order to have 50, 000 or more to live and move easily and efficiently throughout this type of building, new types of elevators must be built. These elevators must not only move up and down rapidly but they would have to move from side-to-side and even forward and backwards. In addition, to various electrical or magnetic rail systems, generators, heating and air-conditioning systems and of course telecommunication systems with built in Satellite systems for entertainment, e-mail and Internet connections.

When nuclear fusion was first successfully produced, an unexpected energy wave was produced, at first it was channeled into huge dummy loads. Then later back into the main energy chamber and recycled as clean power. This was the final technology needed to finally and permanently protect the rain forest. This Nuclear Fusion Wave (NFW) can travel up to 250 miles; scientists and military researchers harnessed these waves and created energy fences. They found a way to funnel this energy between two towers and create a regenerative feedback loop utilizing massive wave-guides. The only draw back to this energy fence is the harmful effect it has on human tissue at close range, for if one is closer than 10 meters to the fence the heat causes severe burns. What is not commonly know is that this effect can be minimized with proper modulation or worsened by injected RF energy.

14

Exodus

Now since the people of South America could not be trusted to protect mother earth, something had to be done about it. In the past, it was neither possible nor practical to remove the entire population of a country let alone all of South America. That is now a thing of the past.

Shortly after Tokyo's Millennium gate was built, and the advent of cold fusion things started moving into place, plans of to evacuate South America, the building of numerous Ms and the creation of a high tech energy barrier that would completely surround the entire continent. The Brazilian fence would enclose much more than Brazil of course, it starts roughly 10 miles inland and goes through Venezuela, Colombia, Ecuador, Peru, Argentina, Brazil, French Guiana, Suriname and Guyana.

The coastal region around the fence is used for scientist, environmentalists and researchers. These scientists and researchers are now able to study the rain forest, look for new cures to diseases and do not have to worry about tribes, local government or the timber industry. For in the past too many scientists, researchers and environmentalists were killed while protecting and studying the world's largest rain forest.

Now that the indigenous people are no longer clear cutting the rain forest, it is slowing growing back, although a great deal of extinct plant and animal life will never be able to be recovered.

According to the governments of the world, pollutions is down, air quality is up, because the rain forest is now saved, mother earth is now producing the necessary oxygen for all the people of the world.

It was propagated that when the Brazilian Exodus takes place, these people would be in better living condition, educated and properly indoctrinated on taking care of mother earth.

The darker side of this exodus was that most people did not want to move, from those in the Amazon to those living in larger cites such as Rio Janeiro and Buenos Aires. Since very few have the chance to visit even the coastal areas of South American continent, due to restrictions, it is not commonly know that most of the area is filled with high security military bases, not just research centers. In order to enforce the no trespassing laws, drastic steps were needed. Satellite surveillance, infrared detection devices, military patrol aircraft and well armed and trained extraction teams. These teams rapidly swept through areas and removed everyone, if they run or try to elude these extraction teams; they were executed or left to die from their injuries. The rain forest and its abundant life, would take care of all those who were killed.

Politics was another factor allowing South America to become one large biosphere, but without the sphere. For by removing all the people it would eliminate a large source of drugs, no people in Columbia, there would be no one to *harvest the coca leaves. People turned a blind eye to the atrocities necessary to eliminate all drug cartels, for the world would be a better place without all the drugs pouring out of Columbia. The environmentalist's rhetoric was to replace the coca plants, or just allow the rain forest to naturally cover all the land.*

It was through the use of high tech military equipment, political expediency that the last remnant was be removed and an international army was formed, Bio-zone Enforcement (BZE). The great majority volunteered to relocate; either under the guise of helping the environment, or helping their families to live a better life or just simple because of their vanity. For humanity has always falling into the trap of status, what better status than living in an M.

The world has not changed; for not every M was the same, for the rich truly lived in futuristic comfort and class, deluding themselves to "Their Brave New World". The poor and those forced out of their homes and off their land lived in modern ghettoes. Sure, they were in a city of the future but there was no rain forest for them, no strolls with natures and no freedom of wide-open spaces.

No one asked himself or herself "if the drug cartel were destroyed and killed and Columbia's coca fields are no more, why was drugs abuse so rampant in the poorer Ms". The poor were still being exploited at the hand of the rich or for political expediency. Revenue from the world government's drug business helps fund continuing research for new medicines that will benefit the upper-class, and to offset the cost of policing the entire continent.

Only the best and brightest moved out of these towering ghettoes and into sparking towers of heaven. The truly rich and powerful still live in huge estates that sit on rolling acres of pristine groomed gardens of hedges and roses with sparkling springs flowing through their property.

At first there was a huge television campaign to encourage everyone to move to a near by island nation such as Trinidad, Jamaica or Cuba and even the Falklands islands. This media blitz showed former indigenous families living in pristine Ms in various bio-zones around the world, which encouraged countless South Americans to be part of the Brazilian Exodus. There still was not enough Ms to house the entire world yet; the lucky were able to move to Trinidad and Tobago or Cuba or to one of the Virgin Islands. The affluent moved to the tower of their choice, but the poor and tribal people were not so lucky. Many of the tribal people of the Amazon who were not killed were shipped to the Australian outback, for why use Mother Earth's valuable resources on them. For these millennium towers needed productive and educated people, to live and run them. In time, there would be a modern place for all the people of the world to live in but not just yet.

In the early days of this great endeavor between the massive media campaign and prior to military intervention the entire world began an embargo. No food or goods were allowed into or out of South America, in addition the World Bank and the IMF stopped providing loans and support. No nation on the earth provided any type of monetary or humanitarian aid for that matter. All this was done to convince the governments of Venezuela, Colombia, Argentina and Brazil to move out willingly. Many felt living anywhere was better than becoming buzzard and insect food. The next phase was a blockade, no ships or aircraft in or out of South America, unless it was ships and planes full of participants of the Brazilian Exodus. It was a small price to shot down aircraft or sink ships violating this blockade, for the greater good would be achieved, "Mother Earth saved and oxygen for all"!

*****

Over all with the advent of the Ms being built world wide, there are more and larger national parks, game preserves and botanical gardens, pollution has gone down and so has crime. For the vast majority of the population of the world now live and work in an M-city, which are connected by subway and monorail systems. As the public transportation systems finally improved and the use of fossil fuels diminished and major "zones" are connected by NSST (Near supersonic transports) rail systems, highways were removed and green belts were established. The auto industry has converter to either building various rail systems or 'Ms'. For there are major populations zones in every country and NSST are the only way to travel between each of them. There are only a few international airports, which SSTs are authorized in and out of, a person would have to fly out of LA and land in Tokyo or Paris and then take a NSST to your final destination. No one is allowed to live outside of these population zones, except those involve in farming and agriculture, the concept of "city towers" had allowed for more room for farming and for cattle and natural wild life.

Just as there is the dark side of the Brazilian exodus, the same applies to all countries that enforce "zones". Extraction teams sweeps through these countries to forcibly remove families or individuals from rural areas back to a zone. If one is lucky, they are moved to environmentally friendly population zones. Friendly because it is not drug infested from

20

the Pantheism drug cartel nor is it a rundown zone of squalor where most of those from the exodus were relocated. Just like in South America, those who resist relocation are hunted down and killed like dogs. Convicted criminals, who were not executed, are shipped to a non-friendly zone, once someone has been extradited from a Friendly Zone like Modern Seattle to a zone of squalor they are electronically implanted and may not ever return. By the off chance they do return to any friendly zone, they will be executed, there implants would release a deadly toxin.

This is not to say that law-abiding citizens cannot leave their zone, no on the contrary all zones have plenty of open spaces for recreational use, such as hiking, fishing, canoeing, sailing and even camping. Those living in rural zones or taking scenic trips must use a hybrid vehicle, part electric and part solar. Swimming in the summer and skiing in the winter are still popular. There is plenty of room for various sports activities and team sports, unless it requires gasoline, for powerboats are banned and so in NASCAR (not big lose there) and motor cross. Professional sports are still popular, there is still a Super Bowl, World Series, The Stanley Cup, the World Cup is still # 1, some things never change for the Cubs, and the Mariner's still have not won the Series.

It is very common to see families taking leisurely walks through all the green belts that replaced all the freeways or doing some gardening in the various community gardens.

Some of the more exclusive Ms own their own greenbelt, where each tenant has a small plot for a garden or flowers, just as the apartments of old each tenant had their own parking spot.   It is almost a requirement to have ones' own garden in the greenbelt, for these towers are so tall that the windows are designed not to open and the required architecture does not allow for any balconies. For these mini-cities in a building have to be able to withstand wind, storms, earthquakes and other forces of nature.

With an increase in natural habitats lots of different animal species have made a dramatic increase.   There are now wild herds of buffalos, roaming free, along with timber wolves, cougars and bears.   Although there is an increase in natural predators in various regions, there is still a slight need to keep the deer and moose populations in check. Hunters pay a hefty fee just to be put in a lottery to get the opportunity to hunt. Each year the game animal may be different and your area may not have any hunting that year depending on the EC's animal preservationists annual report. Northern Canada and Alaska is consistent, while Minnesota and the Pacific Northwest vary. Only select groups of hunters are allowed to hunt and those who illegally hunt or exceed their limit or break any of the regulation dictated by the EC will be shot, literally.

******

It is interesting that a slight raise in temperature was good for the Vikings but catastrophic for the 21st century. Also, note worthy was that for most of the 20th century Chicken Little was calling for the next ice age.

Nuclear Waste

One of the ongoing problems facing humanity is what to do with all the nuclear waste from the old outdated nuclear power plants and nuclear reactors from nuclear submarines and aircraft carriers, along with all the un-needed weapons grade plutonium and uranium. Although Mother Earth is not entirely 'weapons of mass destruction', free.

At first all, this waste was slowly being shipped and stored on the moon, but there was discovered to be mineral ore on the moon, which is needed to build more Ms. It was determined to be cheaper to launch the stuff to the sun, where it would be burned harmlessly up. The problem with this was that not all the spacecrafts could make it past Mercury due to the heat from the sun, solar flares or just solar wind and either crashed on the planet's surface or became adrift in space. Scientists were unsure if continual explosion on Mercury might shift its orbit or cause unwanted debris hurling toward Mother Earth.

The terra forming of Mars had just begun with planting high altitude plant life on the various mountains of Mars and soon other plant life would be introduced to help produce oxygen. For once oxygen levels increases so would the temperature and in turn the ice at the poles would melt slightly, providing water. In an hundred years or so Mars might be ready for colonization, therefore nuclear waste there or on one of its moons was out of the question.

The next option was creating large cargo ships to transport all the waste to Jupiter, then just release the nuclear waste cargo containers and let Jupiter's gravitation pull the waste into its self. Problem solved. Mother Earth and humanity's future is still secure.

December 2025

Radical extremists attempt to destroy the latest M that was being built in Paris was thwarted. New military spy satellites and sensitive sensors were use to find and then track a nuclear warhead from Tehran to Baghdad and finally to Paris. This detailed data was turned over to the President of the United Ecological Community (UEC), swift and severe military retaliation was carried out.

Two stealth bombers took off from a Royal Air force base in England; later they were met with fighter escort from Turkey and finally right before their respective target they were met by two AR-44s.

"Pave way One to central command, request final authorization for nuclear strike".

"Central to Pave way One and Two, Nuclear strike authorized".

"Confirm" Pave way two asked.

"Confirmed by the President, she called herself".

"Bombs away central"

Two tactical nuclear devices were dropped, one on Baghdad the other on Tehran. At the same time, the two AR-44s launched two cruise missiles with neutron warheads at various cities in the region. If terrorist groups do not want to play well with other they would not play. The decision to use Neutron weapons was a simple one, the world needed cities to house all those that will be displaced, either from South America or from rural areas.

******

Not only was this a clear message to the world of the Ecological Community's resolve but it was also a statement that the EC has eyes; their intelligence gathering capability is second to none. In addition, it demonstrates their advance technology, their ability to detect weapons of mass destruction, whether it is chemical, biological or nuclear. 'For Mother Earth is Queen and she has mandated that we preserve her at all cost: Clean Air/Water and the preservation of the species-plants and animals. To sacrifice humanity to protect her wild life is accepted and even demanded, it is our service to her, in return for the natural resources we use to build our cities'.

******

This was the turning point of the Ecological Community finally becoming world government. The future still held many challenges and advancements but with large terrorist states eliminated and humanity becoming enlightened to Mother Earth's mandate, the goal of protecting and preserving the entire world's rain forests will one day be achieved.

In order, to be a truly global society there can be no secrets, nor subterfuge, to do this one's identity must be know along with one's location. With the advent of GPS technology one's exact location on the planet can be known, it is the positive confirmation of a person's identity. DNA is the concrete and irrefutable to one's identity.

****

Global Wireless Tokyo

Information technician Yatomoto noticed extra data being received from all the incoming cell phone calls. The normal data consists of all their subscribers' data, the normal date and time, plus whom the subscriber is calling or receiving a call from, in addition to which cell tower first received the signal from. The nearest cell towers for both parties are transmitted digitally to Global wireless as GPS coordinates. However, the IT tech noticed additional data was being automatically routed to a remote server, which he could not access or even determine its purpose.

"Hey Mr. Whitebear, could you take a look at this"?

"What do you got going"?

"There is all this extra data being routed to server RD&N, and I am not sure even if this server is on site." "I would like to know what gives".

"Lee I know you are a great tech, but since you were just transferred up here you are most likely unaware of marketing's' need for demographic and users' preferences".

"In a nutshell, whenever a user makes a call marketing gets the time they call, who or more importantly what type of business they called. Where they called from and where they call to, meaning did they call from home or from work. Which M-City they called to and from, for example: the user called from New Chicago to New Tokyo. Moreover, did the use sent *text, use voice and the standard video-to-video connection.*

"Did the user access the information network, and if so what type of information was accessed, such as weather information, movie schedules, or was music or video downloaded. Further, more what genre of music or movies as accessed. The list goes on and on".

Yatomota, "Isn't this an invasion of privacy".

No came the response, "it is part of the service agreement and this data is only used to improve the product. This data lets us know what features the customer wants, uses and which geo-zone is more apt to access racy video or technical data. This and all the other data collected is used to determine which areas need more cell sites, towers or larger broadband or improved data transfer rates."

Lee thanked Mr. Whitebear and went on with his work, feeling completed satisfied and believing he learned something.

The truth of the matter was that the RD&N had very little to do with research and development but with DNA data collection. For not only do all cell phones come with embedded GPA chip but with DNA scanners. Every time a person picks up a wireless phone built in scanners starts attempting to get the users' DNA from the salvia via the microphone and through the skins on the key pad.

This data is transmitted to a search and destroy server, for if known terrorists, dissidents and/or criminal makes a call their identity if verified and location pinpointed. This aids in the apprehension of the criminal or the elimination of the terrorist.

****

Paradox

Well, it is a verifiable fact that the chytrid fungus is the cause of the distinction of certain species of frogs, however the cause of the increased bacteria in the atmosphere is what is up for debate.

Please Explain.

It appears the increase of greenhouse warming is through methane emissions, but here is the kicker-new forests may be to blame. Our researchers report that living plants produces 10 to 30-percent annual global methane production. Since most man-made methane and other greenhouse gases have been eliminated with the advent of Cold Fusion, then it is nature that is to blame for the increase of methane.

Wow: to attribute the prevalence of the fungus to global warming has been stymied by the simple fact that higher temperatures are known to inhibit fungus growth -- what a conundrum, a "climate-chytrid" paradox.

What has to be determined is how to cover this up, put a spin on it, and more importantly how to get the Global Community, and the EC to allow for a reduction of plants to decrease the amount of methane gas, and without being executed for heresy.

It was nice working with you all.

Yea, nice to have known you, ha, ha, ha.

Water

On the out shirks of San Diego on a remote urban home used by the head zoologist for the San Diego Wild animal park a group of EC officers arrive to arrest Dr. Parks.

"Dr. Parks you are under arrest for allowing your trees to die".

What! There is a drought out here if you haven't noticed.

That does not matter it is your responsibility to ensure the plants entrusted in your care are watered, even if you have to cut back on bathing or even you drinking water. You know Mother Earth mandates it. You are to protect her at all cost. Now come along quietly Dr. Parks.

Dr. Parks: "This is downright absurd; you think that I killed someone or something".

EC: "Careful now doctor, you do not want to be charged with blasphemy now do yah. For as you are well aware of crimes against nature and Mother Earth are more serious than crimes against humanity".

Mrs. Park: "Tom I will call our lawyer".

EC: "You do that Mrs. Parks, but I would call a gardener first and see if you trees and shrubs can be saved. For the courts may be lenient on your husband, plus unless you want to be charged as well something has to be done."

All criminals want to do whatever the courts ask them to do, for there are not very many prisons. For way waste time, energy and resource on those that break that law. Most were employed backbreaking work or wherever they were needed for the preservation of Mother Earth, one could be literally sent to Siberia or the outback of Australia if a project needed more workers. Once the project was done a few years later that would go back home. It was like a very lengthy community service project but at times on the other side of the world.

Other criminals, the subversive or those who blasphemed against the Mother would be absorbed back into the Earth, neat and clean. Normally the absorptions were televised, on PPV of course, good entertainment.

2050:

With South America emptied of all humanoids (non-indigenous species) and the rapidly successful bio-zones cities and expanding wilderness, the EC set their sights on more land.

"Sir, Did I hear you correctly?"

"Johnson you hear correctly, the EC has decided to halt the project for the time being."

"May I ask why?"

"It's simple, resources, but they assured me that they are working on procuring more of the material needed for the project and that several research labs are working on new material that would work and be easier to make and of course be stronger."

"What about all the workers, there are thousands on this project?"

"Right now the HR department is working on reassigning them to several of the new bio-zones in Canada. In addition, the EC has a completely new project that will be commencing shortly. Don't ask I am not at liberty to discuss it yet."

In the next few weeks, thousands of the Berlin Strait bridge project were given 'pink slips' and others were reassigned to projects in Canada. The bridge would have been one the biggest ever built, with a huge four-lane highway (in both directions), a subway and pipelines. Both sides had *already started and were well on their way at completing the base structures on both sides when the news was broke.*

"WHY, WHY NOW WHAT IS THERE REASONING" was heard everywhere.

"We stopped building the oil and natural gas pipes that were going to be imbedded in the pipe line and converted to steam. So where is the environmental impact?"

"HEY, now the EC never said they were stopping the project for environmental reasons, but because of materials. Plus it is just halted and will be restarted, they assured me of that."

"Yea right you are just as gullible as the Brazilians" was the comments as the meeting broke up.

EC:

"Gentlemen, it now official the Bering Strait Bridge project has been discontinued. Now once everything is shut down properly and equipment packed away and all the workers have departed, we will begin project Exodus II."

"As you know," said the EC's spokesman, "most of the Eskimos have already left over the years and it will not take nearly as long to remove everyone. Moreover, the energy barrier will not be as extensive. For our goal was to have Alaska (the entire state) a natural wildlife reserve and park, but with no one living there. There will be no oil pipeline of any sort in the state and why build a bridge that only implies vehicle travel. The shipment of good can be done in other ways and more importantly using a different route"

"Yes, Mr. President?"

"Well, sir, Alaska should be cleared out in less than 5 years using our current plan and subtleties. But if we use a plan similar to the Brazilian Exodus it will take less than a year."

"Good, good, let's keep it on the low key side for now, since there really isn't an environment issue at stake, so just give me quarterly updates."

Winter 2051:

By order of the EC, teams of relocation enforcement agents were going through all the Ms and forcing all "married gay couples" to remote M-type cities. With the backing of the EC, police and the military, all married gay and lesbian couples were removed.

"Mr. Jones we are here to remove you and your husband to another city!"

Why? Came the response, with fear and trembling.

"Mother Earth is Queen and the future of mankind demands it. For humanity is at stake, the mortality rate far exceeds the population growth. You may find it hard to realize but we will attempt to explain it to you as you pack your things, a transport is waiting."

"Over the past 50 years with married gay couples, fewer children have been born. At first, you all adopted, but fewer of your adopted children grew up to have a traditional marriage and thus fewer children. Coupled with abortion, resulting is less children for anyone to adopt and finally the 'East' using scientific methods for gender selection. "

"For you see over in the 'East' they only wanted male children, and either aborted the females or in the lab ensure the egg and sperm produce a male child. I know you understand the science behind it. What you may not understand is the fact the Mother Nature designed it so that in every society there is slightly more females than males. Now in China alone there is a whole generation of men, nearly 500,000 with no wives, for their parents used selective reproduction. Now all these men will have to wait at least another 20 years for infant baby girls to come to age. Let us get real here, when all these girls are old enough to start having children they are not going to hook up with 40 to 50 year old men they will marry men their own age or a just a few years older. Now think about, a generation of no children for society tried to 'fool mother nature', vanity run amuck. Therefore, the EC has mandated that all those perverting the natural order of things must be relocated. "

Mr. Jones: "The EC is being very intolerant and hateful"

"Now, now, society let you all do what you wanted for over 50 years now, and what did it get us, a population crisis and humanity being in jeopardy, the entire human race is at stake here. Remember Mother Earth being preserved is our first mandate and the second is the preservation of humanity. Nature is our model and example and our Queen Mother Earth cries out that you are an abomination against nature. "

"Just be glad the EC is allowing you all to be relocated and not recycled and adsorbed back into the earth. You could be give "Community service" there are many new projects in the Extreme Northern Territories. "

38

In addition with the population, diminishing not only is there less workers to work but there is less tax revenue in various general funds and the GCU 'wisdom fund'. This prevents anyone from retiring or if they do, there is no income supplement for them. An aging population and lower birth rates — are the main cause of the long-term problems, for Mother Nature designed all life to procreate and further the species.

Social engineering never works, everyone needs to get with the program, for it is simple as the 'birds and the bees', a man and a woman living together to produce a family. The animal kingdom is Mother Nature's example, insects and all the fish in the sea live out her perfect design. Humanity was following this design for nearly 7,000 years of recorded history but abandoned it for they thought they were more enlightened and spit in the face of the Queen mother and embraced science.

2051

Annual EC brief on the state of Mother Earth.

Emissions levels are drastically down; air and water quality is up. Animal and plant life is steady and improving. The mortality rate is down and live births are up.

However, despite all our effects on a global level the mean temperature of the Earth is falling too rapidly.
Isn't that want we want?

Well, no, for Global warming was no longer a major factor once we eliminated the burning of fossil fuels—with the advent of Cold Fusion. For a while, it seemed like nothing humanity did stopped global warming, and all the scientific data seemed to contradict itself. Some data led to the conclusion that everything from temperature, rain and snowfall were cyclic and uncontrollable. One region would have bitterly cold winter and other an unseasonable warm one or the opposite was true in the summer. Then other data would suggest the possibility of another ice age, for this was the "popular" belief in the 1970's and just 20 years later (barely a tick on the geological clock) the popular opinion was global warming.

That was true and we solved it, one delegate blurted out.

Yes, pollution was a problem and it was addressed, forever since the mid 1970's water and air qualities have improved, and once the global community solved the energy problem and severed its dependence on fossil fuels the world turned around environmentally.

Since the turn of the century there has been a shift in the earth's magnetic field: magnetic north has drifted eastward, along with the Northern lights—Aurora Borealis. Scientists have been studying this phenomenon to determine why; this is when they first suspected that the shifting of the magnetic field was due to the slowing of the earth's core.

For at first scientists scoffed at the slowing of the earth's core and leaned towards the fact that the magnetic field was just reverses itself—a change in polarity, in other words the North and South poles was change. The theory was that the poles due change polarity periodically, every few million years or so. Now if this were all that it was it would not be anything that we could not adapt to or prepare for.

It is already a proven scientific fact that the earth's rotation has been slowing over the past million years or so, and as the earth's rotation slows its shape changes. A fast rotating earth causes a more spherically shaped planted, but when it slows, it becomes more elliptical. When the Earth 'spreads outs' from slowing the end results is increased earthquakes and more severe quakes. Therefore, it is imperative that we study the ramifications of the core slowing and perhaps stopping.

The length of time it takes the Earth, at the present time, to rotate once is 86,400.002 seconds compared to 86,400 seconds back in 1820. The rotation has slowed roughly only by 2 milliseconds since 1820. That seems like an insignificant amount of time BUT over the course of the planet's entire lifetime; it has had very profound effects on the geophysics of the planet. It has caused mountains to rise, earthquakes to occur as I have already alluded to.

From scientific research, study and monitoring it is the conclusion of the EC scientific community that the earth's core will continue to slow and possible stop. The data concludes that there is a proportional decease in the earth temperature with the slowing of the earth's core, which may lead to another "ice age" and serious investigation needs to be done immediately.

What happens if the Earth's core stops completely?

Unknown, perhaps a rapid cooling instead of a gradual one, Some scientists theorize a change in gravity—yes gravity to caused the Earth rotating upon its axis and the revolving around the sun, but they theorize that when the earth's core *stops spin then the earth's rotation will also be negatively affected.*

A slowing of the earth's rotation will cause gravity to decrease and any increase will cause g-forces to increase, both are very serious. Which one is worse, the implications are too great and vast too answer.

An ice age where an average man's effect weight is 200lbs instead of 175, not good, or an ice age where every one a whole lot lighter, sound good but from a mechanical engineering stand point it is a nightmare either way.

Mother Earth may be dying despite man's best and most sincere efforts.

Vegetarian Delight

Bob Gacke you are hereby charge with "Animal-Cide", which carries the death penalty.

"You got to be kidding me, I was only feeding my family, and we were hungry".

That does not matter; it is illegal to consume animals. If you only just killed the animal and not eaten it, you who have been charged with "Animal Slaughter"—a felony but it does not carry the death penalty.

******

In the early 21ˢᵗ century animal, starting with certain pets were deemed as official family member or companions and were given legal rights and standing in the court system. For certain judges determined that chimps and monkey were able to "sign" and expression their feelings. Thus, they were considered sentient being on par with humans; soon this status was given to parrots, dolphins, whales.

44

******

'For Mother Earth is Queen and she has mandated that
we preserve her and the preservation of the species-plants and
animals at all cost. With the legal prescient of animals being at
the same level as humans and the EC's charter, it was decided
that the consumption of meat was illegal, immoral and the
Queen Mother forbids it.

Groups like PETA were ecstatic for all animals have
worth in and of them selves. There for many businesses were
shut down, no more cattle rangers, chicken farms, the raising
of pigs. For it was illegal to eat meat, no reason to raise cattle,
pigs, sheep, no more deer or elk hunting.

At first dairy cows and raising chicken for eggs were legal,
along with catfish, salmon, and trout and such. Crab and
lobster fishing slowly diminished due to all the rules, tuna
fishing was illegal, and the dolphins must be protected at all
cost. If a fisherman accidentally killed a dolphin while using
its nets for tuna he would be jailed for killing a sentient being.

Slowly more and more inroads were made and the
entire planet was required to be vegetarian, for Mother Earth
was above humanities needs for food and above anyone's
religious belief that required either an animal sacrifice or as a

required dish for a religious ceremony—Passover, no lamb
allowed or death was incurred. Even Native American's of the
Pacific Northwest were not allowed to hunt whale as their
ancestors did.

Currently milk and eggs are still legal and certain
types of fish, mainly those from fish farms. The fishing industry
has nearly been eliminated, for using large nets is illegal, and
gas power engines are illegal, due to pollution. Therefore,
fishing is very limited to pier side, from the beach or via
riverbanks. Most of the earth's population relies on fruits and
vegetables along with rice, beans and nuts.

It is a good thing that the world's population has
decreased otherwise, Even Mother Earth could not produce
even wheat, corn, rice, or fruit and vegetable to feed the world.

When policies are politically, motivated and long either
term scientific study is ignored or the "debate" is deemed
"over" before a thorough analysis is conducted all hell breaks
loose. A new religion is born and personal rights and freedoms
are abolished.

It is said to learn history or that is will not repeat itself.
If humanity goes the way of the environmentalist then enter
Nazism and Fascism and those that speak out are
exterminated.

2009:

It is interesting that the truth is finally coming out, which is the global warming was all hype, a political move to remove certain segment of the population out of power and forcibly install another segment. However, in doing so the majority are being ruled by the minority, there are words for such things. What is more disconcerting is the fact that all the global warming news, all the laws and regulations, the various taxes put into place is based on a lie, deliberate manipulation of the scientific facts. The only why scientific facts can be twisted, is by unethical scientist, in the old movies they were call Evil and Mad Scientist. Today they are mainstream, elevated and lauded.

We all need to wake up, question and hold all our elected officials, government agencies feet to the fire. Of course, the main problem is the media, who do no report and most likely are unable or do not know how to investigate and report.

www.ingramcontent.com/pod-product-compliance
Lightning Source LLC
Chambersburg PA
CBHW060650290526
45793CB00001B/478